Earthshine
Mimi Khalvati

smith|doorstop

Published 2013 by
smith/doorstop Books
The Poetry Business
Bank Street Arts
32-40 Bank Street
Sheffield S1 2DS

Copyright © Mimi Khalvati 2013
All Rights Reserved

ISBN 978-1-906613-87-7
Typeset by Utter
Cover image: Earthshine by Leonardo Da Vinci
Printed by printondemand.com

Acknowledgements

Grateful thanks are due to the editors of the following publications in which some of these poems have appeared: *Acumen*, *Artemis*, *Cimarron Review* (USA), *Genius Floored: Alphabet of Days* (Soaring Penguin Press 2012), *Genius Floored: Uncurtained Window* (Soaring Penguin Press 2013), *London Magazine*, *Not Only the Dark* (Categorical Books 2011), *PN Review*, *Poetry London*, *Poetry Review*, *Poetry Salzburg*, *The Critical Muslim*, *The Editor: an anthology for Patricia Oxley* (Rockingham Press 2011), *The Forward Book of Poetry 2013*, *The North*.

smith/doorstop Books are a member of Inpress: www.inpressbooks.co.uk. Distributed by Central Books Ltd., 99 Wallis Road, London E9 5LN

The Poetry Business is an Arts Council National Portfolio Organisation

Contents

5	House Mouse
6	Madame Berthe's Mouse Lemur
7	Sun-Sparrow
8	Sun in the Window
9	Starlight
10	Knifefish
11	Sciurus Carolinensis
12	The Conservatory
13	The Little Gloster
14	Microchiroptera
15	The Landing Stage
16	Earthshine
17	Prunus Avium
18	The Pear Tree
19	On the Occasion of his 150th Anniversary
20	Angels
21	What it Was
22	Aunt Moon
23	Fog
24	Statham Grove Surgery
25	What is Snow
26	The Blanket
27	The Swarm
28	The Soul Travels on Horseback
29	The Overmind
30	Tears

House Mouse

Even the mist was daffodil yellow in the morning sun,
a breakfast slant of April sun that glowed on my banana tip.

And in the shadow of my arm a mouse lay, white belly up
like a lemur sunbathing. Begging she was, paws curled,

miniature paws like nail clippings, hind legs crossed
in a rather elegant fashion, tail a lollipop stick.

Pricked on her shadow, her ear and fur stood sharp as grass
but her real ear was soft, thin, pliable, faint as a sweetpea petal

and her shut eye a tiny arc like the hilum of a broad bean.
Yesterday she was plump. Today she's thin. Sit her up, she'll sit.

You can see how Lennie would have 'broke' his, petting it –
mine weighs no more than a hairball, nestling in my palm

as though it were wood pulp, crawlspace, a 'wee-bit housie'
and she, the pup, the living thing. The baby look's still on her.

And the depth of her sleep. I tuck her into the finger
of my banana skin – a ferryboat to carry her over the Styx.

Madame Berthe's Mouse Lemur

We should have been lemurs, lowering our metabolism
to suit, going into torpor in the cool dry winter months

to save on water and energy. We too should have sailed
on a raft of matted leaves out of poor Africa, out to Madagascar

into a forest of mangrove and thorn scrub, feeding off gum,
sweet larvae sugars, bedding down in tree holes *en famille*.

The very smallest of us, the veriest Tom Thumb, the most
minute pygmy, *tsitsidy*, *mausmaki*, itsy-bitsy portmanteau,

little living furry torch, eyes two headlamp luminaries, front
a bib of chamois, tip to tail – and mostly tail – barely as long

as the line I write in, despite illegal logging, slash and burn,
would survive longer than many folk, especially in captivity.

Only the barn owl, goshawk, to watch for in the dark – raptors
with their own big beauty. But Madame Berthe's Mouse Lemur

is caught in the act – a chameleon clasped in her hands,
a geisha lowering her fan: the smallest primate on our planet.

Sun-Sparrow

Sun, like a sparrow in the house, seeks dustgrounds
small as a handkerchief to play in. Sun-sparrow, house-sparrow,

I give you landing strips of dust on wood, runways
between photo frames, wood-grain and wood-knot roses,

nests of cane and cloth for you to steal, netherlands I never clean
for you to bathe in. Here's a dust bath, look, under the bed,

large enough for you and all your family. Why, even
the numbered hairs of my head, fallen, have lined a nest,

innumerable nests and silver they are, the better for you
to shine in. Come, sun, roost. And here is my skin. Warm it.

Sun-sparrow, didn't Sappho herself have sparrows,
fair fleet sparrows, draw Aphrodite's chariot to wing her plea?

I ask no such thing. But I see you land, on wood, on wall,
take flight again and you, who have your own warmth,

need no streetlight, neon sign to roost in – why flee?
Be sociable, stay awhile on my flaking sill, hop right in.

Sun in the Window

Sun sleeps behind the skyline listening to the city.
She'll write in gold today. Wear pinks and reds.

Wrap up warm and enter always smiling, always
ready to be overlooked, leaning her chin on her hands,

frowning when addressed. And her desire she'll reserve
solely for praise, be it modest as an oculus,

a small round fenestration in a wall, set high
and facing west. Terraced, she'll rest her fingertips

on wooden muntins, angle her glance through windows
splayed in Polebrook or Threekingham. And how

she loves lancets, three trefoil-headed lancets, stepped!
A quiet soul she is, an altar rail around her thoughts,

the silk cordon hooked back on its brass stave.
And shy. But look at what she writes. Outshines

the others, the noisy, vociferous others, any day.
I'd give anything for a glyph from the star nib of her pen.

Starlight

Only the brightest stars were out with a half moon
centred in the sky: a ceiling to learn the names of stars by.

And in the gaps between the stars, milkcarts went to market,
pony traps crossed viaducts, oxen drove sad water wheels,

history trundled by as birds awoke and the distant sound
of a plane winked lights. Her owl flew back to Minerva

as she flashed her shield while, on Apadana's stairways,
processions of bearded guards, Persians, Medes, marched past.

Cedar palaces were torched; frigates, night-fishing boats set out.
Passengers flew like vesper bats straight across the moon,

roofscapes listened for child lovers leaning over balconies,
geraniums grew in the dark. I had never been so happy

and historical. Happy enough to see, holding them up,
stars on the tip of each finger, countable, spread wide apart,

one by one go out as day rose to pluck the first strains
of a Spanish guitar. Then the silver moon went white.

Knifefish

Lit, lit, lit, lit are the estates at dawn:
honeycomb stairwells, corridors, landing lights,

flare paths for passengers flying home.
Three jets like electric fish streak the sky with rose.

Black ghost, ghost knifefish, how many days
since you went abroad, lurking in your murky pools,

locating dawn by sonar, by electric fields alone?
To image your world in darkness – driftwood

casting distortion shadows – no matter how weak
your electric organ, small its disharge, barely a volt,

through tail-bend, waveform, you fire, you feel,
sensing lightning, earthquake, your own kind

turning their dimmer switch up and down,
for this is how you talk. Old Aba-Aba, grandpa,

with your one room lit at a time, feeling for walls,
navigating as surely as in the brightest, highest dawn!

Sciurus Carolinensis

Sun rivers on glass, threatens to mount, blaze
into my sightline so that, heat-struck, I headlong

down to hump squirrelled in the shade below, leaves
moving as I move, as grass moves with the snake.

I am the grey. Born helpless, blind and deaf.
My mother lays me across her forepaws, fetches me

out of a cave, weans me once my teeth appear.
Sciurus names only my *skia*, shadow, *oura*, tail.

I displace the red. Acorn-bred, carrier of the pox,
I infect it with lesions, ulcers, scabs, weeping crusts,

it shivers, shivers, *skia, oura*, and then it's dead.
I mean no harm. I'm no image seared on your brain

only seen side on, tail up, ears tufted like conifer spurs;
no nutkin on a branch, jug on a wall, graphic loop,

no ampersand between presentiment and trace.
Skia, oura, I flicker on the walls of the cave.

The Conservatory

If you keep two blinds down and one blind up
and sit under the one that's up under the skylight

and the Sunday morning rain, you create –
at absolutely no expense – the kind of conservatory

you've always wanted but without the wicker
and kelims, the view on to the dripping garden

and the cat, all soaking, hidden under a hedge.
You are elevated instead. You are a bird in a nest.

Rick as a small boy sold birds for pocket money.
He made his own trap out of a wire washing basket,

a stick, some fishing line, some bread, catching
sparrows, dunnocks and, if he was lucky, a finch,

before progressing to proper trap cages with a call bird
that would sing and attract more birds he'd extricate,

sell, then start over again. Now he's a mouse-catcher
with no pension. 'You're not illegible', he said they said.

The Little Gloster

With such icy winds, facing the rising sun in the garden
makes no difference. So I take shelter on the terrace,

comforted by two black sheepskins, one under me,
one over, kindly provided by the establishment.

Seagulls, seen from below, their red feet neatly stowed,
beaks and eyes painted like wooden toys, hang

immobile long enough to be scrutinised in flight
before they swerve away. Propped against a fence,

a reindeer is spotted with fairy lights you expect to see
vanish like daylight stars and everything that loomed

last night on a smuggler's night black with storm
– the distillation tower's disembodied four red eyes –

retreats into its rightful place. Young waiters, chefs,
preparing for the fair, are lining up white deckchairs

close enough to the sea-edge to feel spray. Sandwiched
between sheepskins, I am half man, half sheep, myself.

Microchiroptera

Only human noises populate the night. No owl, pheasant,
wailing fox, only stars that have buried their heads in cloud.

Listening becomes a momentous task. The eye as always
fights for supremacy and the ear, fazed as a bat in rain,

imagining it hears a rush of water, hears 'all things hushed'.
O *chauve-souris*, flying mouse, leather mouse, flittermouse,

jealous naked microbat, winged seed of sycamore,
umbrella man, acrobat hanging in your own skin parachute,

flying patagium carpet, O bat-being in fairy wings,
string purse, anus face, where are your echoes now

– sweet flutter of a mothwing, rustle of a centipede –
where is your pulsing cry, your lovesong in the dark?

In the vast homelessness of a country night – dear country,
left behind – we come back into our moral being, back

into the animal ground of our being under the absent stars.
Under their roofs and rafters, we navigate that ground.

The Landing Stage

How slippery the path just at the end where the indigo stutters
of dragonflies rain against glass water! Where everything is flower –

the air, its scent, cabbage whites, single, paired; pines, cedars,
carpet dew; where old age flowers in its slow walk to the water;

where the left brain flowers and the right, the lawnmower
sprays grass fountains; where sadness settles for the pinecones,

not knowing if they are really pinecones at this distance;
where Anne flowers in an orange shawl and our lungs

are grey wildflowers, minds a mindless garden; where,
in the event of fire, we are to collect at the bottom of the lawn.

We are to collect our belongings, blankets, iPads, medicines.
We are to collect sunlight silvering on our shoulders.

Our shoulders are thin. We collect our thinness, our boniness,
in a huddle of silver water down by the river. Be careful!

they warn me, those who are, going down to the landing stage
raised high enough to dangle younger legs over the water.

Earthshine

Under the giant planes beside the gate where we said goodbye,
the one bare trunk where squirrels flatten themselves on bark

side by side with a voluminous plane whose ivy outraces branch,
under the two great planes where we stood vaguely looking round

since it was a clear night, the street empty and we, small gaggle,
newly intimate but standing a yard apart, keeping our voices low

though they carried bright as bells as we counted the evening out,
gestured towards the cars, deciding who would go with who

and gradually splitting off, under the planes with the squirrel dreys
hidden in all that ivy, but hanging low directly above the station,

there, where we looked pointing, like an Oriental illustration
of Arabian Nights, lay the old moon in the new moon's arms:

earthshine on the moon's night side, on the moon's dark limb,
earthlight, our light, our gift to the moon reflected back to us

and the duty we owe our elders as the Romans owed their gods
– duties they called pietàs, we call pity – shone in the moon's pietà.

Prunus Avium

We buried my mother's ashes in the holes, the four
we dug to plant four cherry trees for her, *prunus avium*:

wild cherry, sweet cherry, bird cherry, gean or mazzard,
each name carrying something of *prunus avium* on the wind,

the wind that blew drifts of ash like bonemeal across clay.
In three years they'll be grown; in twenty, diamond woodland.

But we'll recognise our trees, set back where the path ends.
Surrounding them will be native oak, beech, alder, hazel.

One cherry tree from each of us: Tara, Bea, Kai and myself.
And on Tom's behalf, we invoked the name of Yax Tum Bak,

Mayan God of Planting, there in a desolate, bitterly windy field
in Buckinghamshire. Clay stuck to our boots in grassy clumps

and as Tara heaved her spade, worms, lustrous as white mulberries,
fled, upturned. Later, in the Garden Centre – 'Oh, how beautiful!'

my mother would have gasped on entering – I bought Tara
a peach tree for Valentine's Day, *Prunus Persica*, from Persia.

The Pear Tree

And when there's no poetry in it, the hour, the sky,
only cumulus and the first faint ossicles of rain

pattering on glass like a bone bundle thrown
for a shaman to divine, when no answer comes,

faith gives up, brain slackens, skin sloughs off
like a turtle shedding old scutes from its shell,

when the same dread incubus squats on the heart,
hiding a breathing hole on the top of his head

for all breath, desire, have long fled his mouth,
when friends disappear – and were they friends? –

and your head on its single stem weighed down
heavy as a baby pear tree not with pome or pear

but with time's three globes, what then,
little pear tree, bletted by frost? A rootstock

has dwarfed you the better to bear but quince,
pear, whose bridal kiss will you perfume now?

On the Occasion of his 150th Anniversary

Let's fling down a cloak of gold leaf on wove paper,
let's do the pavement like Klimt. Like his father

before him, Ernst Klimt the Elder, gold engraver,
and his brother who took up engraving later –

whose deaths in one year were the fount of his vision –
let's do acacia in a shower of coins, engrave each face

with The Kiss. For semen is flowing like golden rain,
double yellow lines meander in gold metallic ink

and the streetlamps are on – *O spark of the Gods!* –
it's snowing gold flake, sweeping mosaics along the curb,

spandrels of gold between car wheels. Werewolves,
gorgons, are sauntering out of their lairs, trick or treaters

with quince-red cheeks and my beautiful girl in a tent
of yellow roses twines her corn snake round her wrist.

As a night fox trots through a gold-barred gate, trapping
gold-dust in his fleece – quick, hammer him into the frieze.

Angels

Updraughts lift sounds of language imperceptibly, even
the silent language of Lula as she hobbles up the steps.

Dogs Lula doesn't know bark along the terraces, cockerels,
though it isn't dawn, crow anyway. It could be any village

anywhere in the world, everything in decay. But things
retain their scent – the rubbed tomato leaf – and sound

– the bamboo river – and as if heard behind closed doors,
the angels: angel of September, of the fallen fig and dapple;

angel of perspective that staggers the terraces upward,
white steps downward; angel of the sister mountains –

the first, the second, the third. And the angels, cowled,
circle us like lepers on the hills, they unveil themselves.

And I love my angels not as they were in childhood,
angel of the crabapple and chine, of calico and sandal,

but as they are: leprous and discharged, violent and betrayed.
Angel of the soft wind that blows across my breasts.

What it Was

It was the pool and the blue umbrellas,
blue awning. It was the blue and white

lifesize chess-set on the terrace, wall of jasmine.
It was the persimmon and palm side by side

like two wise prophets and the view that dipped
then rose, the swallows that turned the valley.

It was the machinery of the old olive press,
the silences and the voices in them calling.

It was the water talking. It was the woman
reading with her head propped, wearing glasses,

the logpile under the overhanging staircase,
mist and the mountains we took for granted.

It was the blue-humped hose and living wasps
swimming on the surface. It was the chimneys.

It was sleep. It was not having a mother,
neither father nor mother to comfort me.

Aunt Moon

Aunt Moon, Old Glamour Moon in a haze of smoke
puffing behind your folding screen, Old Barren Moon

with your round pig belly, what lies, what lies!
I love you for the lies you've told! Lies with a belly

of milk, lies to call the children in, gather them
round your mirror fogged, Old Moon, with death.

No lying now, is there? No creeping round the houses,
sweet Jokester Moon with your pearly teeth, implants

that went wrong, weren't they? One look at the truth
and you vanish. O what a clear clear sky, clear as day!

But I saw you, Moon, in the doorway. Spliced in two
as the glass revolved, in purdah with your back turned.

Who were you whispering to, Aunt Moon? No one,
was there? No one ever to lisp to, bribe, stab in the back,

no one to revenge. For the best lies are told with a bevy
of innocent stars in your eyes, not in a revolution's doorway.

Fog

World is headless, cut off at the waist and we, bundled,
seeing snowflakes only as they pass across a face,

we earth-dwellers who know heaven's a cloud, a bank,
an upperwhere, otherwhere, whose cloud deck homes

lure our spirits with lights in the fog, paraffin stoves,
our Bethlehems, our backyards become Bethlehems,

we whose hearts race the blinder we grow, we moles,
we dirt tossers, we mouldywarps with no eyes or ears,

with a mouth at one end, anus at the other, we pipes,
we cylinders, who have stockpiled our subterranean hell,

our mole runs, underground galleries, larders for a clew
of earthworms, we labour of moles with paws like rakes –

what have we left but these hands now, we boars, we sows,
with four limbs, one nose, a body plan and a taupe pelt?

World is headless and we, who have only touch and smell,
must touch and smell gas, smoke bombs, blood-meal, bait.

Statham Grove Surgery

Seen in disbelief through fug in the workmen's caff
with its canisters of snow, in the panoramic distance

of Clissold Park wearing its hood of grey wool, chef's hat
in the snow, behind a fallen tree trunk languid as a nude,

a human hare, grey on grey, white gloves, white hind paws,
is shadow-boxing while their trainer, red on grey, holds up

focus mitts for a second sparring jackrabbit, black on grey,
like the hare on the moon. Yellow eyes glide down the road;

horse-chestnuts waltz in whalebone, braceletted with crows;
my cappuccino breathes out smoke. Ruled on park railings,

black is a marriage of scissors and snow. But in Statham Grove,
among red pillar-box hills, gold corridor woods, we turn into

house-plants, umbrella plants, gum trees, rubber leaf hands
green-striped with snow, deaf to a story a young dragon tree

hears, enthralled. Dr. West wears a bright red stethoscope.
Homeward-bound, we leave footprints in a black leaf-fall.

What is Snow

Snow is a rubbing of sorts, a wax heelball on ground,
an impress of ribs – exoskeletons in high and low relief.

Each snowflake is witness to the cloud-womb that formed it,
how wet, how warm, the union of crystals, how powdery.

Trapped in firn, air will evidence ash from Krakatoa,
deposits from lead smelters, pollen and greenhouse gases.

Snow is adjectival. On foliage particularly, discriminates
between the feathery and lobed, the linear and pointilliste.

In itself is silent, but on contact, creaks. Acquires an air
of sanctity in repose but in action earns oaths and profanities.

Snow is a friend to children, those who have scarves, mittens,
tobaggans and wooden sledges. To others, it is the devil's own,

akin to the djinn who frequent sinkholes, wherever mud rejoices.
To the children housed in sheep sheds, chicken coops, tents,

dressed in cut-up blankets, seeing things that aren't there in forests,
snow is the devil they know. Better him than the live bombing.

The Blanket

Cold, yes, under a sodium sky at three o'clock in the morning.
But there's this shawl to wear and tea with Manuka honey.

And across the only gap in the border, a thousand refugees an hour
pouring through Ras al-Jedir. An hour? By morning, my morning,

another five thousand, by lunchtime, another five and how many
have even a striped hemp blanket? Fifteen thousand blankets!

Imagine one. The way it folds stiffly as a tent around the head
bent back, the shoulders jutting, knees drawn up, wrists free,

the lone triangular edifice. Feel the weave. Hairy, ridged.
Smell it. Determine the sightlines either side of the hollowed cheeks.

Imagine the scene in silence, not as it would be. The blanket
as a block, a wood carving. The tools: straight gouge, spoon gouge,

back bent, dog leg, fishtail chisels, V-tools, punches, vices;
hook knives, drawknives, rasps and rifflers, mallets, saws, abrasives;

slip waterstones – how quiet they sound – and strops for sharpening.
Figure in a blanket. In acacia, sycamore or, most likely, olive.

The Swarm

Snow was literally swarming round the streetlamp like gnats.
The closer they came, the larger they grew, snow-gnats, snow-bees,

and in my snood, smoking in the snow, I watched them.
Everyone else was behind the door, I could hear their noise

which made the snow, the swarm, more silent. More welcome.
I could have watched for hours and seen nothing more than specks

against the light interrupting light and away from it, flying blind
but carrying light, specks becoming atoms. They flew too fast

to become snow itself, flying in a random panic, looming close
but disappearing, like flakes on the tongue, at the point of recognition.

They died as they landed, riding on their own melting as poems do
and in the morning there was nothing to be seen of them.

Instead, a streak of lemon, lemon honey, rimmed the sky
but the cloud-lid never lifted, the weekend promised a blizzard.

I could have watched for hours and seen nothing more than I do now,
an image, metaphor, but not the blind imperative that drove them.

The Soul Travels on Horseback

and the road is beset with obstacles and thorns.
But let it take its time for I have hours and hours to wait

here, snowbound in Lisbon, glad of this sunlit café
outside Departures, for an evening flight to Heathrow.

Being my soul's steed, I should like to know its name
and breed – a Marwari of India, Barb of North Africa,

the Akhal-Teke of Western Asia or a Turkoman,
now extinct? Is it the burnt chestnut colour of the ant,

grey as a Bedouin wind, the four winds that made it?
O Drinker of the Wind, I travel by air, sea, land

and wherever I am, there you are behind my back
pounding the cloud streets, trailing banners of cirrus

or as Platero once did, from fear or chill, hoofing a stream,
breaking the moon into a swarm of clear, crystal roses.

No, no matter your thirst, ride swiftly, mare, stallion,
mother, father, for without you I feel forever homesick.

The Overmind

Even when I was a child, tears were something
other children had – a permission I didn't understand

other people gave, I thought the children gave it
to themselves: a special treat when they'd already

had their share. My overmind as H.D. called it
isn't a jellyfish, a kind of swimming cap on my head.

My overmind seems to be this sadness – I nearly always
carry it and it *is* a kind of hat, skysize, skyshape.

I feel sorry for my smallness, short trunk, short legs,
sleeves rolled up, feet too large to be in proportion.

When I sit and plant them neatly, side by side like shoes
with no one in them, I feel how flat they are and firm.

If I were a pot, a round ceramic pot with a mustard glaze
on a whatnot in the guest room or on an outside table,

I'd be, like H.D.'s Delphic charioteer whose feet made
'a firm pedestal for himself', I'd be always balanced.

Tears

In the first weeks after my mother's death,
I curled up on the side of my heart like a foetus

and wept. My tears were like water, sweet and clear.
They flowed of their own accord, soundlessly,

while my body, my mouth and even my eyelids
lay as peacefully as in sleep and the more tears flowed,

the more I wanted them. World was foetal then.
But in the weeks that followed, tears dried up

and world took up its stick and walked blindly
through the riverbeds. Had they been floodplains,

had there been no dams to render them obsolete,
nilometers would have measured the overflow

from faraway monsoons on stairs, pillars, wells.
Too high and there'd be famine, too low, the same.

I measured distances by her. My mother my compass,
my almanac and sundial, drawing me arcs in space.